PLAYWRITING, Brief & Brilliant

by

Julie Jensen

CAREER DEVELOPMENT SERIES

Smith and Kraus, Inc.
Hanover, New Hampshire

Published by Smith and Kraus, Inc.
177 Lyme Road, Hanover, NH 03755
www.SmithandKraus.com

Selections from this book have appeared in
The Writer and *The Writer's Handbook.*

First Edition: November 2007
10 9 8 7 6 5 4 3 2 1

Cover and text design and book production by
Julia Gignoux, Freedom Hill Design

ISBN 978-1-57525-570-5
Library of Congress Control Number: 2007937068

CONTENTS

Introduction

My favorite book on writing has always been Strunk and White's *Elements of Style.* They lay it out for you simply and directly, and they do not go on. You feel confident when you read that book; you don't feel overwhelmed or discouraged. So I've tried to do that same thing for playwriting. I've laid it all out for you without going on.

I have just one suggestion before you begin. If you're inclined to write a play, you might want to read this book quickly, write your play, then read it again more carefully. It is definitely not a good idea to make yourself nuts with requirements, then try to make your play fit them. Tell the damn story. Then let this book help you fix it.

Dialogue

There is supposed to be a study somewhere claiming that more people have tried to write a play than have tried to write a story, a poem, a song, or a novel. It seems that would-be writers have been seduced by the idea of other people saying their words out loud. They wanted to hear their ideas spoken by good actors to an audience of eager listeners. This is, of course, a fairly problematic reason for writing a play, even though it does suggest what people focus on first, namely, getting someone to talk. We will begin, therefore, with dialogue, a playwright's great friend and eternal nemesis.

First let us remember that dialogue is action. It is not treading water, it is not swimming backward, it is not thinking about swimming forward, and it is not standing on the side of the pool deciding how it might feel to dive in. No. It is in the water and swimming forward. That means I discourage my characters from talking about what already has happened or what might happen. Likewise, I forbid them to talk about how they feel about what did or might happen. Right away someone is going to raise her hand and ask, "Yeah, but what about exposition?" That leads us to the next truth.

Disguise exposition. A piece of expositional dialogue, which is only exposition, should be cut. Expositional dialogue should, therefore, have at least one other function besides exposition, besides telling us what has happened before the play began. Perhaps it furthers the conflict, complicates the plot, or raises the stakes. I always make sure it does something else, anything else, but sit there and explain the past.

If I follow this little dictum, I magically rid my play of some early writer awfulness. For instance, characters don't ever say the words, "I remember," and that is a blessing. Likewise, one character never has to tell another character something they both already know, such as how many children they have, where they live, or what year this is.

The other secret about exposition is not to off-load it all at once. Sprinkle it around. That gives me a better shot at disguising it. I always choose to risk obscurity rather than flat-footedness.

Third on the list is fairly obvious. Characters should sound different from one another. That's just another way of saying no two characters are the same. Playwrights ain't Noah. They don't take on characters two by two. They take them on one by one. Each must be unique and different. They might all have the same accent or speak in the same dialect, but that doesn't mean they are alike. Making them sound different is an early test for making sure each one is unique.

Next on the list is one so important that it should be first. Characters should want something from a scene. And what they want should be pretty specific and definable. What's more, those wants should be at least slightly at odds with the wants of others. This sounds pretty crass, since I hate people who always want something from me. But characters are not people I take to lunch. They're more calculating than that. When they don't want something pretty specific, they just wander around. The scene they're in is a floater, as useless as dead seaweed.

Finally a dietary suggestion. Make dialogue lean. As lean as you can get it. Dialogue is a racehorse, not a mule, not a work plug, or a fat mare in the field. When I finish a scene, I take after it with a pencil. I try to get it down to its essence. Sometimes that's too lean, then I'll allow a little more flesh. But I don't want fat. The trouble with fat—on the body or in a play—is that it's more of the same. I like the idea of putting dialogue on an exercise program, to keep it moving and keep it lean.

Now the reverse layup. Sometimes dialogue is not spoken. I try to give characters the option of occasionally saying nothing, and doing something instead. There is, for example, a reason why Nora's door-slam at the end of *A Doll's House* is such a memorable moment. She has nothing more to say, and what she does is infinitely stronger than anything she could say. As playwrights we often get caught in the web of believing that saying is all. Well, it isn't all, not anywhere near all. It's just talk. Doing something often has greater power. And besides, it keeps directors, inclined to discount stage directions, on their toes.

As I finish up this list, I realize that some of my so-called dialogue rules are character rules. I trust you will excuse me if I occasionally confuse them. But characters are what they say and of course what they do, dialogue merely one of the conveyances.

****

CHECKLIST ON DIALOGUE

- √ *Dialogue is action.*
- √ *Exposition should be disguised.*
- √ *Characters should sound different from one another.*
- √ *Characters should want something.*
- √ *Dialogue should be lean.*
- √ *Sometimes dialogue is not spoken.*

Character

We'll start here: characters should be interesting. Of course, folks sometimes groan and complain about that. Interesting is hard to define, they say; it's different for everybody. Well, I don't agree, but just in case they're right, I fall back on a fairly trustworthy dictum: characters have to be interesting to me.

That puts me on the spot: I have to take responsibility for my characters. And as a result, I'm less likely to let them wander into tedium. It's a little like taking your cousin to a party. You don't want her to fail because that would hurt her feelings and you like her. So you ask her good questions, laugh at her jokes, and, in general, encourage her along. That's about as far as the cousin metaphor goes, though, because you do get your characters in a whole helluvah lot of trouble. And you're supposed to; it's your job. If, however, the rest of the items in this checklist are in place, you can blame their troubles on the characters themselves, and that's a lot nicer.

What follows, then, is a character checklist. Not all characters have all the items on this list. But my best ones have most of them.

First, they're off balance in some way. They're excessive in one direction, deficient in another. And they are tenacious; they don't easily give up their imbalance.

I used to have a test for characters called the Othello test. Could my character hold her own in a play with Othello? I mean, that man was off balance! And he was also tenacious. He was capable of believing big and acting big. If my characters could pass the Othello test, I knew they had enough stuff.

Second on the list, they gotta want something. You've heard that one before. But it's true, and true things are worth repeating. Therefore, they gotta want something.

And they also gotta want something specific. It's not quite enough for Hamlet just to want something big like revenge; it's also important that he want something in the moment like to convince his girl friend he's nuts. This moment-to-moment goal helps move things along and prevents a scene from dangling or floating.

Third, they gotta have a well-defined rhythm or tempo. That helps me imagine how they would move as well as how they would tell a joke. But moving is the critical thing here. Characters need to be moving. For my money, they should be working. We are, after all, a very busy people. We don't sit around and carry on long conversations. We catch things in quick bites.

Next on the list, they have blind spots. This might be the same thing as a fatal flaw, except less cosmic. Blind spots are the habitual behaviors that result in both tragedy and comedy. Willy Loman wanted to be well liked; that's his fatal flaw. He wanted it so much that he lied to himself and others. Habitually. That's his blind spot. Ralph Cramdon on *The Honeymooners* couldn't stand to lose; he would always overcompensate when he was in danger. As a result, he'd get himself in even more trouble. Blind spots enable a character to move from zero to sixty in a single breath. Think of Archie Bunker in *All in the Family* whenever a liberal issue is mentioned. It's like a man hitting a patch of ice on the sidewalk. A blind spot will always trip him up. Blind spots are automatic responses; they make characters funny and tragic.

Next, characters, like the rest of us, have always just come from somewhere else. And when they were there, they did something. That means that characters come to any scene with some baggage, with an attitude. I don't want them to explain where they've been or what they did. That would violate the dialogue rule about exposition, but as the writer, I want to know where they've been and what they've done. It always affects the opening of the scene, no question, but it also affects other things too: rhythms, tempo, attitude, patience, innumerable other intangibles.

I also like characters who surprise me, who surprise themselves. Surprise, by the way, is one of our best weapons, far too underused in my opinion. Writers generally are a bit too preoccupied with consistency. Characters are set up then, and their choices become predictable, the outcome overdetermined.

Remember the laughing scene in Beth Henley's *Crimes of the Heart*? That scene becomes the climax of the play because it is so surprising. Likewise Sam Shepard's errant brother in *True West* stealing all the toasters in the neighborhood and toasting an entire loaf of bread. Nick in Adam Bock's *Swimming in the Shallows* falls in love with a shark, then the shark goes to the beach with him and to a wedding. The audacity of these scenes. We are delighted and gratified.

Now a human truth and also a character truth. Characters, like the rest of us, almost never tell the truth. Sometimes they're protecting themselves, sometimes they're manipulating others, sometimes they've got a skewed vision of the world. And sometimes they're just polite and go along when someone else seems to know more. When I remember this little dictum, my plays are also saved from another early writer problem: the character who knows everything and tells all. In other words, I am saved from writing myself into plays, that witty but put-upon, sensitive but all-knowing asshole.

Which leads us neatly to a suggestion that characters ought to have a nice mix of traits. I like my characters smart about some things, funny about some things, and eloquent about some things. God forbid, however, that any character should be smart about all things, funny about all things, or, worst of all, eloquent about all things.

Finally, I like characters best when they cannot help but be themselves, when I as a writer just have to relent and let them do their thing. That's such a nice feeling. I like to imagine Shakespeare's delight at having created Falstaff, then just farting around while the son of a bitch went wild in front of him. I would like to have been there.

Before we leave this subject, I need to remind you that this is a checklist for major characters only. If you make all your characters this complicated, you'll give your play to Fortinbras. Too much complication in a minor characters can be a dangerous thing.

****

CHECKLIST ON CHARACTER

- √ *Characters should be interesting.*
- √ *They should be off balance.*
- √ *They must want something.*
- √ *They have a definite rhythm and tempo.*
- √ *They have blind spots.*
- √ *They have just been somewhere and done something.*
- √ *Characters are surprising.*
- √ *They don't tell the truth.*
- √ *They have a mixture of traits.*
- √ *They are what they are, in spite of themselves and you.*

Plot

You have no doubt had the experience of sitting for long periods in front of a piece of writing trying to decipher it. We all have. We've all been subjected to Serious English Daze.

Serious English Daze has an attitude about plot. It is not discussed. Serious English Daze explains with a sneer that it is cheap and very unserious to discuss plot. Serious English Daze likes the works of James Joyce, Samuel Beckett, and a host of young men who went nuts in foreign countries. They like to decipher works of LITT-ra-ture.

So that means that if you are a writer coming up in these times and you're studying English, as you should, you've learned that texts are poured over, as if they were sediment in a river laced with gold. You imagine a scene hundreds of years hence. Some English students are going over a piece of yours. You see the students struggling with it. You see the teacher smirking. You are yourself smirking. Because you will have written great LITT-rature. So great that a room full of native English speakers cannot understand it.

Now then, because you know something about this game and you are very serious, you might write to be deciphered. Terrible mistake! Quit it, and quit having fantasies like that.

First of all, plays are heard and seen but once. They must communicate in real time. No chance to stop and ponder. Second, it is a terrible mistake even to try not to communicate. Third, plays and works of art in general communicate emotionally; getting intellectual on your end of things is a mistake. Leave that to the Serious English Daze.

Now on to plot. These days plot is more important than it used to be, because it does go in and out of fashion. During the Albee, Pinter, Mamet era, it was less fashionable. Beckett had influenced these writers, as had a lot of other so-called Absurdists. Without ever saying so directly, Absurdism fostered the notion that good writing was plotless, that, in fact, plots were a thing of the past. Even so, the best writers of the period and of the movement were very good with plot. And it is a good idea for writers to develop that part of their craft.

The first way to think about plot is that it answers a question. Will Hamlet avenge his father's death? Answer: yes, but he'll die doing it. In *Waiting for Godot*, will Godot ever come? No, not today. Will the guys in *American Buffalo* make a fortune off the buffalo-head nickel? No. Will Jesse in *'night, Mother* kill herself? Yes. They're simple questions, they don't involve interpretation, they're straight out. But they are what compel us through to the end.

What's more, this question that the play poses needs to be clear by the 10 percent point. So if your play is 10 pages long, we need to know the question by the end of the first page; if your play is 100 pages long, we need to know it by page 10.

At about this same point you'll want to accomplish something else—the inciting incident. That's the event that gets it all going. If your play is a football game, the inciting incident is the kickoff. It is not the coin toss or the sweet expression on the faces of the players during the National Anthem. It is what gets things moving and does so strongly. After the Ghost visits Hamlet, the play has been kicked off; after the guests arrive at

George and Martha's house in *Who's Afraid of Virginia Woolf?*, the play has been kicked off.

Now to the rest of the plot. The easiest way to work on plot is to keep asking yourself, "And then what? And then what?" That keeps you focused on events and outcomes. And it keeps the story moving.

Another way to think about plot is to ask the Stanislavski character question: what does the character want, and what will she do to get it? Stanislavski was an actor, but this question is good enough to suggest that he could have been a writer.

His question also implies the necessary element of conflict. And no plot is possible without it. Even though it's against our higher moral instincts and runs counter to the way we want our lives to be, conflict in all its myriad possibilities is simply essential to plot, so there.

When I was first studying this issue of plot, I heard over and over again that a plot had a beginning, middle, and end. I never could understand that. Everything has a beginning, middle, and end. A flat line, a knotted thread, a piece of sidewalk. And yet none of those is a plot.

A plot looks to me like a long slope up a hill. The climax is the peak. As you progress up the long slope, however, there are several impediments or plot points. Fences and forests, rivers and riots. Your job is to decide what the fences and forests, the rivers and riots really are. Then space them out. You've got yourself a plot. Here's how it works. Hamlet wants revenge. He's walking the long upward slope of revenge. A lot of fences and forests: Ophelia is one, Polonious another. A lot of rivers and riots: Gertrude is one, Laertes another. At the pinnacle is Claudius himself. These plot points are challenges or complications, things that impede the progress of the hero or heroine, things that cause danger, things that go bump. These things get bigger as the play goes on. Then by the end, either the things win or the hero does. And that's the plot.

A guy I used to know in television, a sitcom writer, said that a plot was getting someone up a tree by the first commercial, throwing things at him till the second commercial, and getting him down by the end. That's a plot all right. *Hamlet* has the same plot, only in that version Ophelia, Gertrude, Polonious, Laertes, and Claudius are all apples.

Now there are a couple more refinements for this plot picture. By the halfway point or somewhere thereabouts, I like to put a big X. That's the point of no return. After that point, the character can't go back. After he's killed Polonius, Hamlet can't go back. After Martha's gone upstairs with the biologist, she can't go back.

Finally, the resolution occurs after the climax. The climax answers the question, and the resolution is a moment of quiet, a settling in, getting used to the answer. In *Hamlet* the question is, "Will Hamlet get revenge?" The answer is, "Yes, but he'll die too." So the settling in is Horatio's speech and the Fortinbras stuff.

A settling in does not need to take very long. In a shorter play, it can be a quiet line and a pause. In a sitcom it can be joke. But it can also take as much as a whole scene. As it does in *Hamlet.*

Now then, the parting words about plot. If you sat down and told a story, you would know instinctively how to tell it. Plot structures are instinctive structures. Writing a play is the same. Go ahead and tell the story. Later, after you've finished, think about the structure. Writing isn't a recipe business. It is more inventive than that. If it's cooking at all, it's trying to put together a good dinner from what's left in the fridge. Challenging, demanding great originality.

But really, it's more like telling a story to some friends, hoping they'll think the same things you did: that it was funny, that it was sad, that it was infuriating, that it was a relief, that it was a damn shame. So go ahead, write your play. Then pick up these notes and figure out if there's something you'd like to change.

****

CHECKLIST ON PLOT

√ *Plot answers a simple question.*

√ *The question should be clear by the 10 percent point.*

√ *An inciting incident gets things rolling.*

√ *Ask yourself, "And then what? And then what?"*

√ *Ask yourself,"What does the character want and what is he doing to get it?*

√ *Conflict is a necessary part of any plot.*

√ *A plot looks like a long path up a hill with obstacles along the way.*

√ *The point of no return is reached by the midway point in the play.*

√ *The climax answers the question of the play.*

√ *A resolution or settling in occurs after the climax.*

Sets

I once did a playwriting workshop with a bunch of grade-school kids—from which, of course, I learned far more than anyone else. When I let kids loose to create a play, the first thing they thought about was the set. And if I let them, they would have built the set, the entire and complete set, before they ever made the play—any of it. For them, theater was the set.

This serves to tell us something about the importance of sets. We instinctively build houses, houses for our plays, houses for ourselves, our families.

The trick here, for ourselves as well as the kids, is to keep it simple and keep it controlled. An audience would much rather *imagine* a fire on a ditch bank than look at a light under some sticks. They'd rather imagine a pickup truck from two chairs and holstein seat covers than from any amount of paper, paint, cloth, or metal.

Playwrights also need to cover their butts. Frequently their work is done without benefit of a budget. They themselves need to know how their play can be staged simply and effectively. We should not have to see the actual ascending light, the giant elevator, and the smoke effect to be moved by what happens at the end of your play.

In fact, the best theater in the western world did not have the benefit of a lot of sets. The Greek playwrights and Shakespeare thought very little about sets. They used the same space for every play and told us where we were. The medieval era and the nineteenth century, two rather dreary periods for theater, thought a lot about sets. If this little example serves, one should give oneself a set like Shakespeare or Aeschylus or Thornton Wilder and go at it.

Having issued this invitation, I'll provide some cautionary notes. Beginning playwrights tend to overvalue the verbal elements of their craft. After all, we are called writers. But the important thing to remember is that we are working in a genre that is also very visual.

People in Hollywood like to say that film is one-quarter verbal and three-quarters visual, that television is half and half, and plays are three-quarters verbal and one-quarter visual. That might be right if you average it out over the course of a whole play. But at some moments, a play is 100 percent visual. So if that part of the play is ill-conceived, it can also be failing at 100 percent. A disastrous thought!

Here are some things to think about sets. They gotta be interesting to look at. And that includes elements of beauty, detail, style, proportion, function, simplicity, and color. It includes all the things you learn from studying visual art. And so I could send everyone off to study art, and that's not a bad plan. A stage at any moment is a picture. And it always says something. It's important we know what that is.

As playwrights, we need to open our eyes. We need to pay attention to the entire and complete visual aspect of our lives. If you have only three folding chairs on the stage, make sure they are in the right places. Make sure they are saying as much as they can.

Here's a little list of suggested activities that you can do in your regular hang-about life:

Look at rooms, look at spaces. Think about what kind of play goes in what kind of space. Think about what a space or room says about character.

Look at nature. Remember nature.

Look at furniture. Look at architecture.

Look at people. At people moving. People working. People sitting, lounging.

Look at your own spaces. Where you live, where you work. Do your spaces reflect your personality, your mood, your work?

Rearrange rooms in your mind. Think about how to make them say something very specific. How could you say, for instance, that the people of this house have just gone off to a funeral? How could you say that these people have small children?

Study every space you're in for its visual elements. And then, even more important, study every space you're in for its emotional elements. How does that space make you feel?

Finally after you've done all this, think about the possibility of setting a play someplace other than a kitchen or a living room. Plays need to take place where we live. We live less and less at home. Those evenings are long gone when we would sit around in the parlor and talk. Let's presume, however, that you're greatly wedded to the idea of a kitchen or a living room. Your play is a kitchen or living-room play. Set the play in the "living room" area of a mall. Think of the marble bench, the outsized plants, the endless tah-dah of the music. Suddenly you have a play that is more volatile.

Moving the play to a public space will immediately affect its tempo. A quicker thing is going on here. There are folks around. Anything can happen.

Normally a two-person play settles on a question of who will win. When the setting suddenly opens up that question, you've got a much fuller plate, many more than two possibilities.

Think about sets that provoke and surprise. I set one of my plays in front of a manger scene. The plywood wise men wearing purple and green poster paint, the plywood sheep larger than Saint Joseph, a yellow cardboard angel stuck up on a piece of lath, and all the characters surrounded by bales of hay. This set was loaded with a lot of weird and complicated meanings, not least of which was the fact that whatever was seen by the audience was also seen by baby Jesus.

Sets influence every aspect of a play, from tempo and rhythm to character and plot. They're great fun to contemplate.

****

CHECKLIST ON SETS

- √ *Think simple.*
- √ *Trust the audience's imagination.*
- √ *Notice how nature arranges things.*
- √ *Notice how people arrange them.*
- √ *Study furniture.*
- √ *Study architecture.*
- √ *Note how spaces reflect character.*
- √ *Note the emotional and expositional clues in a set.*
- √ *Think about setting your play in a surprising place.*

Image and Issue

These two ideas don't really belong together. But as words they fit very nicely, so we'll cope. I also don't have very much to say about either one of them, even though they're both hugely important. Image, in case you can't remember from some class or another in LITT-ra-ture, is a literary device that appeals to one of the five senses: touch, taste, sight, smell, or hearing.

Images make a play turn over in the pit of my stomach. They appeal to something deeper than the story or the characters. My imagination is challenged, my soul is touched.

In my best work, the images come quite naturally. And yet I've found that consciously thinking about them is a good idea. It definitely helps when I'm stuck. If I make a list of images that go with the setting and the situation, with the people and their emotions, I usually discover something that ought to be happening.

A comedy of mine, *Thursday's Child,* is about a contemporary family in great and dangerous chaos. It's like February in their lives. Far from spring. Mud. Gray cold days. Coats. Wind. These images suggest events. Ken is sick with the flu, Marcy can't find her coat, the dog comes in with muddy feet.

Images are good, deep, and trustworthy things. The deeper, more primeval they are, the better.

Sometimes when I'm stuck, I like to write into the image. In other words, I take image as the play's reality. That assures a more visceral experience and sometimes means the plot is sharper, character less predictable.

I consciously wrote into the image for a scene in *Two-Headed,* a play of mine about polygamous nineteenth-century Utah. The leading character has just learned that her husband will marry again. She's furious. I made a list of all the images that described her. Trapped was first on that list. And so I put a trap in the scene. In a rage, she swings the trap in the air and it catches her own hand. The image, therefore, became an element in the plot instead of just a figure of speech.

One parting idea on the subject of images. Our culture overvalues the sense of sight. That's one of the reasons I like to stress the other senses. What, for example, does fright taste like? To me it tastes like vinegar because vinegar scares me.

This is by no means all that could be said about images. But one thing's sure, if I said anymore, I'd be repeating myself. And therefore, on to issue.

Issue is what a play addresses besides itself, what it represents beyond its literal story. Think of the play as a light, think of the issue as what is illuminated by that light. *Othello* is a play about a racially mixed marriage. But that is not its issue. Its issue is jealousy or obsessive love.

For me as a writer, issue is what bothers me, what pisses me off, what troubles me in my life. Issue is the sand that irritates the oyster. (Oops, I've just called writers oysters!)

Back to issue. If a play is about the Holocaust, the issue might be something like racism, primitive instincts, or violence. It might also be one of two equally opposite things like triumph or loss. *Bent* is a play about the Holocaust, but its issue is triumphant love.

Likewise the same issue might be represented by radically different stories. Fugard's *Master Harold . . . and the Boys* is a play whose issue is racism, even though the same story could have had a different issue, had Fugard so chosen: warring generations or neglected children, for example.

Issue is what keeps a writer interested in plot or character or any of the other parts of a play. Issue is how come a writer can finish a play. Issue overcomes the burden and the boredom of writing. Issue sustains us through the thin and thicket of plot.

In *Last Lists of My Mad Mother,* my play about a mother-daughter relationship, that's the plot. The issue, however, is dementia and what love looks like in the face of it.

Finally, let me say that issue is a fully conscious part of writing. It is not part of the mysterious underbelly that can be called right brained. It is completely and totally in the sun. It is part of the discourse of our times, and plays must necessarily participate in that discourse and with as much intelligence as possible.

P.S. It is necessary to add this postscript. In America we like to believe that art and politics are separate. They are, however, not separate and can not be separate. When Wendy Wasserstein ends her play *The Heidi Chronicles* with the tableau of the art historian rocking a baby, she enters into the dialogue on women's roles and says something fairly specific about choices women make. Likewise, Albee enters into the dialogue on marriage and Shepard on the corruption of the western myth. These discussions necessarily have political implications. We cheapen theater, limit the playwright, and lie to ourselves when we say that art does not address the political. Even in trying not to imply the political, a writer speaks volumes. Might as well admit the truth and be smart about it. Yes, Gloria, the personal is political.

****

CHECKLIST ON IMAGE AND ISSUE

- √ *Images appeal to one of the five senses.*
- √ *Writing into the image makes a figure of speech literal.*
- √ *Working with images other than visual yields more originality.*
- √ *Issue is what a play is about besides its characters and their story.*
- √ *It is a fully conscious aspect of writing a play.*
- √ *Issue might be political, moral, or philosophical.*

Sound

When we think about sound, we are not necessarily thinking about meaning. And yet when we consider spoken language, meaning and sound are inevitably connected. But I'm proposing here to separate language from meaning, to consider the element sound as its own entity. Sound is a right brainer, meaning a left brainer. Hence, writing plays is particularly difficult because it mixes up left- and right-brain activities.

And so to sound. A play is sound and pure sound. It exists as much in the musical realm as it does in the visual. For me finding the right sound is the most satisfying search. Going after the fewest number of words to say the biggest thing, finding those very words, and then hearing them said right, sung right—that is one of life's great pleasures.

I like to think of writing as drumming, the writer as the drummer. That's particularly true if the writing is meant to be said aloud. Hence, some poets (not many) and all playwrights are drummers. Nice job if you think about it.

Sometimes I think of two characters as drummers. In and of themselves, they each have a rhythm defined by how they move, how they speak, how they feel that day. They likewise connect or collide in a rhythmic way.

Think about capturing the rhythm of a writer like O'Neill, the endless undulation, repetition. He seems to be in a rocking boat. Compare that to the rhythm of a playwright like Mamet, a machine gunner. Or think about Pinter whose famous pauses scare us precisely because they fail to carry through on their rhythmic promise.

Occasionally an actor will say about a line that it can't be read, it's hard to say. That's another way of noting that the musical or sound element of the line is off. In return, playwrights cringe and complain about actors who paraphrase lines. It's not that the meaning has changed but that the melody has. I remember my first experience with an Equity production of one of my plays, and I had to sit through eight hours of rehearsal everyday. I left each afternoon exhausted from having put body English on every misread line. I was trying to recapture the rhythm, the melody of the original line. It had nothing to do with missing the meaning; it had to do with missing the beat.

An editor friend of mine, a graceful writer in her own right, claimed that every sentence she wrote imitated the cadence of another line in her head, that of some other writer. The idea seemed strange to me at first, but I did understand what she was saying. Once I adjusted to the idea, I had to admit that sometimes I heard and imitated such lines myself.

Certainly we all play with builds, the length of the build, and the implicit musical elements in that. That's a beginning. The trick is to be aware of the element of sound throughout.

Otherwise, do I do fancy-ass things like imitate sonatas? No. Do I know one Italian word for any kind of musical thing? No. Do I know that emotions have tempos, people have them, too, and that all things have their rhythms? Yes. And do I care about that? Damn right!

****

CHECKLIST ON SOUND

- √ *Plays function as pure sound.*
- √ *Dialogue can be percussive, undulating, or a hundred other things.*
- √ *A build contains implicit musical elements.*
- √ *Characters and dialogue both contain musical elements.*
- √ *Awareness of the musical elements in a play is essential.*

So What Comes First?

It doesn't matter. It doesn't matter what comes first. Sometimes it's character. Sometimes it's story. Sometimes it's issue. It could also be a sound or an image. It doesn't really matter which is first as long as by the end all of them have been engaged. You can't write a good story without a good character, you don't have a good character until you have a good story. And your play is not good anyway without an issue.

For me the impetus for a new play is usually the issue, something I'm thinking about, or more probably, something I'm having trouble with in my own life. Frequently it's something that pisses me off.

The issue then goes in search of its characters. I have a collection of characters hanging around in the barroom of my mind. To all of them I have said, "I'm gonna use you someday." But the truth is that by the time they're finished and in a play, the characters are amalgams of several people I've known, together with a healthy dose of my own invention. They are not lifted completely from my life, but they are influenced by people I've known.

Story comes next. And that develops slowly. It begins with isolated scenes involving characters grappling with the issue. And it develops from there. Once again, the material of the story is not autobiographical for me. The issue might be, the rest is not. At this stage I like to work with collections of images because they are visceral.

I typically write dozens of scenes in quick succession. I know that most of these scenes will eventually end up in the play, but at the time I'm writing them I do not know where. I feel very free, at this stage, to wander all around, experiment with all sorts of places, character combinations, and styles. It's fun, I'm excited, I feel like a genius.

These scenes are often short, sometimes only a beat (the equivalent of a paragraph in a work of fiction). I'm working on a theory of little pieces, big pieces. It's hard for me to imagine whole structures, especially at the beginning. But it's easy and effortless to imagine little ones.

When I have a few dozen pages, maybe twenty or thirty, I try to put some kind of order on them. I know there are big gaps, but I try not to worry about them. I'll fill them later. Sometimes I discover that I've started my play several different ways. That doesn't trouble me. I'll figure out later where to begin. Sometimes I discover I've written the same scene over and over with slight variations, different augmentations. That doesn't trouble me either. I know from the repetition that this is an important episode in the play.

At this scene-sorting stage, the play is teaching me about itself. Another way to put it is that the unconscious is teaching the conscious, or the right brain is teaching the left brain. This is a more difficult stage than the last and not nearly as fun. The trick is to keep an open mind and not get judgmental or, god knows, discouraged. If I remind myself that I'm just trying to learn what's here, I find I am more creative about solving problems, filling gaps, and finding order.

The last stage is when I let in the editor. She is not altogether pleasant. She's kind of an exacting bitch, if you want to know the truth. And for that reason, it's important to keep her out for a good long time. She'll turn the genius into a retard if I let her in too soon. But she is necessary. She is good at cutting things, good at patching holes, good at perceiving structures, and she has a wicked sense of rhythm.

Here's an example of how it works for me. Several years ago, I was going through a bad patch. I was frightened by a lot of things. Job security being the biggest. I couldn't seem to get a hold on this fear, and it was doing bad things to me, such as paralyzing my imagination. I had an issue: fear.

I needed characters. I got myself a little old lady from my hometown in Utah, someone a little judgmental like my grandmother, a bit strange like my piano teacher, very nervous like my mother. She was a frightened lady.

Next, I needed a story. I began to mess around with some things that would frighten this woman. I moved a house full of people in next door. Strange people, deformed people. The kids, all too numerous, were noisy and way too friendly; the mother was quiet, slow, and threatening. The images proliferated: night, water, blood, strange children's chants, silence, breathing, death. I even came up with a cat that had no hair on its tail. A wondrous image, as it turned out, and one that eventually yielded an entire scene.

And so I worked throughout the play to scare this woman to death. Her task was to survive, both herself and the folks next door. It wasn't easy, but she did accomplish it. And that was my play.

As an ancillary note, I will tell you that living through this woman's fear also helped me put my own terror in perspective. That's not to say that writing must or should be therapeutic. But for me, it is like watching friends wrestle with a problem. I learn from that as I learn from my plays.

I suppose at this point I should admit that I don't use outlines. For me the trouble with an outline is that I piss away the inspiration on something that's not the play, and I end up writing predictable stuff. The spontaneity goes. I always want my characters on an edge in every scene. I want to keep forcing decisions from them. If I already know their choice, I am likely to write a scene that is overly determined, stiff, simply not alive. On the other hand, if I give my characters their head in every scene, I discover their depth, their dimension. I also discover that the outline is useless. So why have it at all?

Now I feel compelled to add that many good writers I know *do* use outlines. It's certainly a more economical way to work. And if you ever end up in Hollywood, you have to use outlines. That's how execs get a say in your work. You will also need an outline or something akin to it if you're applying for a grant or a commission.

Well, that's how it goes for me. Except I also need to add this. Every time I write something, I think it's going to be easy. I'll just dash it off. But it is never like that, never even close. Writing takes time and a lot of work. And every time I'm just a ways down the road on a new play, I realize that I'm in a dark forest in a foreign land. Quite lost, without anyone to ask directions from, and without the language to ask, even if there were someone there. And so, despite my neat little process, sounding so clean and precise, it's never quite as simple as this, because every play is different, has to be different. If I do the same thing twice, I'm dead.

****

CHECKLIST ON WHAT COMES FIRST

√ *I usually start with an issue, something that troubles me.*

√ *Characters come next.*

√ *Then I write several dozen short scenes.*

√ *After a few dozen pages, I see what's there and find an order.*

√ *Then I let the editor in to fix it, fill holes, and make the story work.*

Writer's Block

I remember talking with a friend about nuns and how sad it was that the orders were dying out. She, who was herself a nun, said, "Well if they die out, they should die out." I thought that awfully crass. Endangered species, after all. But then I found she thought the same about writing, and she was a writer. If you could not write something, then it should not be written.

Now that was unthinkable to me. I had always regarded writer's block from one vantage point: its cure. What other points of view were there? Well, there's always the point of view of a tree . . .

And there's the historical point of view. When I look at my own work, I discover that the things on which I was most blocked were also the least interesting when finished. They were so damned proficient, but without ignition. Is it possible that writer's block is sometimes—only sometimes—telling us something? And might that be to shut up already?

That's a pretty disturbing thing to hear. What if writer's block were telling us something a little nicer? What if we valued it, encouraged it? What if writer's block were a great blessing, a wonderful gift? An award from the writing gods, greatly coveted, announced by people in gowns on live TV?

If it were so considered, we'd actually use it right. We'd use the time we're not writing to do something really interesting. (Watching TV, doing the dishes, or finishing the taxes would not be good enough.) We'd do something we had never done before, something we had always wanted to do. We'd have an adventure, even if only for an hour. We'd reward ourselves instead of beating ourselves up. And guess, just guess, which one encourages creativity?

Now that was a sneaky way to begin, but it is the first suggestion for the treatment of the condition, and what follows are some other suggestions for the cure.

Tell yourself you're just making notes. Remind yourself, no one is going to read this. And remind yourself as well that it's easier to fix something than nothing.

Automatic writing. Give yourself a set amount of time. For beginners, two to five minutes is enough; later you might want to work up to ten or fifteen minutes. During this time you do not stop writing, not even if you repeat the same word for a whole line. You keep writing, and you try not to censor. You also don't worry about making sense or telling a story. You just write. When you finish your allotted time, you will likely discover that you're no longer blocked.

The next suggestion I learned rather late in life because I spent too many years in school where people simply do not get enough sleep. After I was out of school, I found that writing first thing in the morning was best for me because I was closer to an unconscious state. Right-brained time. I don't have breakfast, don't take a shower, don't make a phone call—god knows, I don't make a phone call. The phone is one of the biggest impediments to writing. That and, of course, e-mail.

I also have the most luck when I know what I'm going to do next. That means that if I'm interrupting work just to make tea, I want to know what I'm doing when I come back. And it also means that at the end of the workday, I'm better off if I prepare for the next one. And maybe the most helpful of all, before I go to sleep at night, I try to think about what I'm going to do the next day.

Read. Marsha Norman claims to read four hours a day. I don't do anywhere near that. But I've always found that reading gives me ideas, always, never fails.

Surprise yourself. Scare yourself. Be radical and daring. Make yourself laugh. Make sure that you are, in fact, writing something that entertains you, interests you, something you think is important.

Interestingly enough, when I've been the most blocked, I've found that I was trying to make something work, trying to finesse it, but really I was lying. So tell the truth. Get off your horse and walk on the ground.

Finally we need to realize that every writer has two people inside. One is a genius and one is an editor. The genius is the writer, and in order to do her work, she must believe that she is writing the greatest play ever. Later when you've got a chunk of material, you can invite the editor in. He will tell you that you're hopeless, but that he can help you. Never let the editor in before the writer has finished. Never.

Last on the list, consider writing something else. I have, for example, just finished writing this little booklet because I'm blocked on two other plays.

****

CHEAT SHEET ON WRITER'S BLOCK

- √ *Do something else enjoyable and unrelated.*
- √ *Tell yourself you're just making notes.*
- √ *Try automatic writing.*
- √ *Find your best time of day or night to write.*
- √ *Know before you quit what you're going to do next.*
- √ *Read.*
- √ *Surprise yourself, scare yourself, be radical, daring, funny.*
- √ *Write something else.*

Thinking Like a Playwright

Being a playwright is a helluvah way to make a living, but it's interesting otherwise. The best thing about it is that your life is always important, not because you use it, per se, but because paying attention to it is vital. And the best thing about paying attention is that it keeps boredom from the door.

If I were you, I would not become a playwright if I wanted to be either rich or famous. And I would not become a playwright if I needed a lot of positive regard all the time. On the other hand, being a playwright is good if you like public humiliation now and then, and if you are good at swallowing hard and going on. In other words, playwriting is high-risk behavior.

The theater is a collaborative art form, don't forget. Your work depends on the contribution of several other artists. If they do not live up to your standards, your heart will be broken. It's bound to happen, no matter who you are, no matter how well you write.

On the other hand, making theater is an act of immense generosity. Nowhere else do you find the energies of so many focused on the pleasure of so few. Everyone involved is dedicated to doing the best they can. And still sometimes, more often than not, things don't work as well as you imagined, as well as you wanted. At those times it's hard not to blame someone. It's human nature. And yet the writer needs to think on England and endure. It's not a good idea to blame or blow up. The world is too small, and playwrights' power all too tenuous.

Sometimes, on the other hand, this collaborative business works better than you could have imagined. And on those rare occasions, when it really is that good, you need to breathe deep and enjoy. Whatever you do, though, don't project that feeling into the future. It is what it is in the moment and no more. Just because this production worked does not mean that the next one will, that the reviewers will like it, that your life will turn around. It means only one thing: a good production that night, amen.

Frequently I'm asked to give someone an appraisal: Do I think so-and-so can make it as a playwright? That's really a stupid question to ask me. I don't control very much, first of all. And second, what does "making it" mean? My best advice is to see as much theater as you possibly can, imagine new ways to use the stage, and write plays that you want to see, plays that are not like anyone else's. After that, you need to be tenacious, sweetly tenacious. If you've done and been all of the above, you'll still need a healthy dose of luck. After which, you and I will both be asking, what does "making it" mean?

Finally I'd like to say something about time. Writing takes an enormous amount of it. And it is almost all time alone. No one else is either necessary or helpful. Giving yourself enough time is important.

Playwrights often get in trouble with other theater people who are the most gregarious folks on earth. Their entire working lives, after all, are spent in the company of others. They look at time alone as time wasted. Writers, on the other hand, think of time alone as a gift from the gods. The best time in their whole lives is spent alone—if only they could get enough of it, they'd have a career.

What's more, a writer needs to feed that part of his soul that is alone. One wants to write from a source comfortable with itself. Spending time alone and liking it is important, a necessary prerequisite for the job.

I have found that I write best in short intensive spurts. That means that having several days in a row where I don't have to leave the house is valuable. Many people can't manage that. But they can manage an hour every morning. Or all day Sunday. And so it is our business to understand how much time it takes and then protect the necessary amount of it.

For that reason it is most important for all writers to learn these words: "No, I'm sorry, I gotta work." We need to practice them over and over. We need to figure out how to say the same thing in a thousand different ways. No words serve us better except the ones we put on pages. And now if you'll excuse me, I've gotta work.

****

CHECKLIST ON THINKING LIKE A PLAYWRIGHT

√ *Understand that playwriting is not about fame or wealth.*

√ *Although theater can be magical, don't project beyond the present.*

√ *See as much theater as possible, use the stage in new ways.*

√ *Write plays you want to see, plays unlike other people's.*

√ *Feed the part of yourself that likes to be alone.*

√ *Discover under what circumstances you write best.*

√ *Learn how to excuse yourself from others so you can work.*

Format

Here's the format you use for a play manuscript. It does not look like either a film script or a published play. It does, however, look like the manuscripts that actors work with. And everyone's used to it. So you probably should not try to improve it.

> *(Scene setups, descriptions of things, indications of movement, anything that isn't dialogue goes inside parentheses and is usually italicized. Every line of it is indented and single spaced as you see here.)*

CHARACTER NAME

Dialogue goes here. It extends to either margin. Note that there is a space between stage directions and character name. Also note that the character names are capitalized.

OTHER CHARACTER'S NAME
The other person's dialogue goes here. A space comes between the dialogue of each character.

(Stage directions, surrounded by parentheses, go here with a space before them and after them.)

That is absolutely all you have to know. There are a few other fancy-ass options, but they're mostly affectation. For example, in the stage directions some people capitalize all the letters in the names of the characters. Nothing wrong with that, except it's harder, and you need to be consistent. Sometimes you can put acting clues inside the passage of dialogue. That's fine. *(Italicize them, put them inside parentheses, and use them sparingly.)*

One other important thing is that plays should take about a minute a page to read out loud. Test yours to see that it does.

Now something about the other pages in your manuscript. The title page ought to contain the title, your name, address, e-mail address, and phone number. You want people to be able to get in touch with you. You also want to include the date the play was written and the copyright symbol ©.

Copyright is more important for film than it is for plays. (Hollywood even copyrights ideas.) In the theater there is less money and less paranoia. I have never heard of anyone in the theater getting in trouble over stolen material. Nonetheless, you want to be professional, and the copyright symbol indicates that you know your rights. Putting the copyright symbol and date on the title page is called an informal copyright. That is all you need most of the time, particularly if a few other people know you wrote this play and can testify to that effect.

Another alternative is something called poor man's copyright. That involves sending a copy of your manuscript to yourself, then not opening the envelope when it arrives. The postmark establishes the date, and the contents, your work. You simply keep the sealed envelope and if ever there's a problem, this is your evidence.

If your play is published, you will want to get a more formal copyright. For that, you write to Copyright Office, Library of Congress, 101 Independence Avenue, SE, Washington, DC 20559. You can also get information and forms from their website: www.copyright.gov.

On the second page of your manuscript, include a list of the characters and a phrase describing each one. Be brief. On that same page include a few sentences about setting. Again, be brief. For example, describing the setting as a kitchen in a 1950s tract house is probably clear enough, particularly if you add some character specifics like it's excessively clean or there's a basketball hoop on the fridge. We can imagine the rest. Generally it's the job of the playwright to suggest vividly, not to describe in detail.

Some playwrights like to throw terms around, "The door down right leads to the archway up left center." Save your words. If someone wants to do your play, they'll do it whatever way they can do it. There may or may not be an archway up left center. And that probably won't matter.

Besides which, you have to be mindful of other people's jobs. Directors move people around the set. So they might have some good ideas about placement of doors. Designers put things in their places, decide exactly what those things are, and what they look like. Your job, then, is to enable other people to imagine well.

Finally, on that second page of your manuscript include a brief synopsis of the play, about a paragraph long. This angers playwrights, I know. We figure if we've written a whole damn play, that's enough. Well, it ain't. The synopsis will help you if you write it well. It will also help a theater describe your work to others, including the press. Practice the craft. Be brief and try to make your play sound interesting enough to turn the page and read on. A good synopsis can also help you get grants. So you might as well learn how to do it and do it well.

Above all, you want to be mindful of your readers. You want a lot of people to read your play. You want some of them to be collaborators. You probably don't want to show off, indulge yourself, or seem difficult to work with.

****

CHECKLIST ON FORMAT

√ *Follow the sample at the beginning of this chapter.*

√ *Make sure each page takes about a minute to read out loud.*

√ *Include name and contact information on title page.*

√ *Copyright your play, one way or another.*

√ *Include list of characters, setting, and synopsis.*

The Rewrite

Rewriting is like milk or exercise, either you like it or you don't. Also like milk and exercise, it's necessary. So it's best if we all learn to like it. Better yet, if we all learn to love it.

That said, it's wise to be open-minded about rewrites. The best playwrights listen to advice from others: friends, directors, actors, designers, dramaturgs. Then they cull the suggestions and make the changes they find genuinely helpful. Unwise playwrights take all suggestions and try to incorporate every one of them. Foolish playwrights listen to no one and make no changes at all.

Here are a few suggestions, things to keep in mind during the rewriting process.

The first concerns plot. Ask yourself this question: What's the difference between the characters in the beginning of the play and at the end? In other words, did something happen? Think back on your favorite plays. Compare the leading character at the beginning with the one at the end. Look at Romeo and Juliet when we first meet them. By the end, of course, they are dead. But they have done more than just die. They've gone through a lot. And that's good. One sign of a good plot.

The second test concerns structure. Are the events in an arc? Arc implies an arch. Can you picture your play's events neatly arranged on a slightly off-center archway, or better yet, on that mountainside? Make sure you can name each of the events that make up this structural arc.

The third suggestion concerns character. Go through your play very carefully, one time for each character in the piece, becoming a different character each time. The object is to make sure the character is doing and saying what's appropriate to him. You want to take his side, believe what he believes, even if he's an Iago. You're trying to avoid turning your character into a pawn of the playwright, doing and saying things necessary to the plot, but not honest to himself.

Next, make sure you've written beats. Beats are the small units of a play. They correspond to paragraphs in prose. It's easiest to define a beat as the time between when a character starts to pursue a goal and the point at which he achieves it, changes it, or stops. That section or segment is a beat.

Sometimes a piece of stage business is a whole beat. The character reads the note, thinks a second, wads it up, and tosses it into the fire. That's a beat. A beat might also be a page or two long. A woman wants her husband to wrap a present for their child. Her pursuit of that goal is a beat. Her reasons comprise the elements of the beat. She's running late, she's got to change her clothes, and the child will be home at any moment. When she grabs the box, tosses it on the couch, and decides to wrap it herself, that's the end of the beat.

The reason you write in beats is simple. You want your play to be made up of sections rather than isolated lines. It's also easy for actors to play beats. They understand them instinctively and will endeavor to supply them if you don't. The structure of the action is also easier to apprehend if it's divided into sections.

Now then, a radical suggestion: Don't think about expanding your play. Think about shortening it. In general, playwrights worry entirely too much about their work being too short. Most people in the audience worry about a play being too long. Try packing a lot of events into a small amount of time rather than scattering a few events over a long period of time.

Adam Bock's play *Swimming in the Shallows* is about 70 minutes long. David Mamet's *Glengarry Glen Ross* is about 90 minutes as are Harold Pinter's *Old Times* and *Betrayal.* Caryl Churchill's later work is all short, in the 70- to 80-minute range. Two of my most successful plays, *Two-Headed* and *Last Lists of My Mad Mother,* are 75 to 80 minutes long.

In general, there's a growing trend toward shorter plays, which are produced without intermission. Theater experiences need to be intense. Audiences just won't put up with a lot of talk. They certainly can't put up with boredom. And overlong plays threaten both.

Cut any scene not necessary to the story. Even if it contains some of your favorite lines, what I like to call kittens. Yes, kill your kittens. If a scene doesn't further the story, if it sticks out as "writerly," calls attention to itself or the writing, that's a no-no. The writer equivalent to a showoff child. Embarrassing rather than impressive.

Cut also any repeated beats, any section in which the character repeats the same tactic in pursuit of the same goal. Say, for example, a character wants his sister to leave the room. His first tactic is to lure her out, his second is to insult her, his third is to threaten her. If he threatens twice, it is less effective than if he threatens her only once.

Now we move to the micro-editing stage. Pare down the individual lines. Make sure they're economical. What if a character says something like, "Oh, hell, Bill, how many times do I have to tell you? You just don't understand anything." Maybe it would be better if it read, "Bill, you ain't got a clue." Make sure you've tested every line for economy. Almost always, the most economical version is the best.

One final suggestion. I like to apply this one after I've been playing with the details, the mechanics, because it is a marked contrast. Test your play for truth. Is what you're saying true? Is what this character says and does true? You can learn to finesse anything, but make sure you don't lose your soul in the process. All the technical expertise in the world can't compensate for a play that lies.

****

CHECKLIST ON THE REWRITE

√ *Make sure the characters have changed during the course of the play.*

√ *Try to make an arc of the events in the play.*

√ *See the play from each character's point of view.*

√ *Make sure you've written beats.*

√ *Think about shortening the play.*

√ *Shorten individual lines.*

√ *Make sure your play is true.*

Developing Your Play

Development is a word, more importantly, a concept, that is loaded with fear and loathing for many playwrights. In general, their complaints are easy to understand: (1) there is too much development and not enough production; (2) some plays get developed to death; (3) development can yield a play made by committee, with little originality, style, or edge. Consider also this comment by a friend of mine, "Development is about sanding. Except that plays shouldn't be smooth. They should be rough, splintery, and jagged." And it's true that many of us have been through or watched development experiences that got carried away.

But there are also hundreds, even thousands of alternative versions, plays that ended up immeasurably better after development work. Tony Kushner's *Angels in America*, for example, was developed by several different labs and theaters over a number of years. There is little doubt but that the plays that came out the other end of that process are much better than the plays that went in.

American theater invented new play development; no other country does as much with it. Beginning in the 1970s, we took on the job of helping playwrights make their work better. Labs and retreats sprouted like crocuses, and many theaters established their own reading series. All promised an opportunity for professional actors, dramaturgs, and directors to help playwrights hone their skills. Out of that interest grew a spate of graduate MFA programs in playwriting, which are, when you think about it, merely protracted and focused development processes. Judging from the development end of things, we might conclude that the American theater is healthier than it's ever been. While it'll take a generation or two to decide whether that's true, what is true is that most other writers are not given the support and encouragement that many playwrights receive. And that's a wonderful thing for us!

I like to think of development like practice for an athlete. A chance to improve your skills with the help of good coaches in a relaxed setting without the pressure of competition or production.

Now here are some suggestions to assure a good development process. First of all, believe what it says, it's a chance to work on your play, it's not an audition for production. If you keep your eye on the prize, you're more likely to improve your play, and that will enhance your chances of production.

Second, the watchword of new play development should be "Take chances." In all aspects of the experience, try to make the most of your time. These situations are working retreats, they're not vacations. They're also pressure cookers, exhausting and intense. Best to dive deep and swim far to get the most from the opportunity.

Next, take seriously the chance to work with professionals. They are accomplished, gifted, and generous, and they have experiences different from yours. They've seen and worked with hundreds of plays. They know the field from a different angle. And they often end up your professional friends and colleagues, people you may work with again, people who can advocate for you and your work to the rest of the world.

Steal what you can. This is the one place on earth where it's legal to steal. If someone gives you a good idea, don't decide not to use it just because you didn't come up with it. This is your play; it derives from many sources, not the least of which are the people hired to help you.

Listen carefully. Then take the advice that seems right, discard the rest. Not everything will be useful, but not nothing either.

Development opportunities give you a chance to get out of your basement and let the light shine on your work. It's a fine way to discover both the limitations and possibilities of the play you've written. You might discover that your play ignites ideas in others whose experiences are different from your own. And that, finally, is what the theater is for.

I can honestly say that some of the best experiences I've had in the theater were in development situations. Good actors and directors can allow things to happen that could never happen otherwise, certainly not in the pressure of preparing a production. These are moments you didn't imagine, could not have imagined. Something so strong that you can be nothing but gratified to have seen it. Such moments are born of passion and generosity from people whose craft is as well developed as your own.

And this leads me to a particular appreciation of mine—actors in development situations. They are among the finest you'll ever meet. They're good at making strong choices, showing you possibilities. They're also genuinely committed to making your play work, not to showing you its flaws. They are often adept at improvisation and can help you imagine scenes not yet written. Finally, they can help you understand your play from the inside—from the actor's perspective.

Related to development but not the same thing are the artists' colonies, free residencies given out to deserving artists and writers. You have your own room and your own studio, and in general, you are not allowed to talk with others during the day. Every effort is made to maximize your time for work. Some people find that time spent at colonies among the most productive of their lives. Others go stir crazy from the silence.

I think everyone should set up their own retreat now and then, even if it's only at the local Motel 6. Give yourself a chance to write without interruption for a period of time. It's remarkable what can be accomplished when the phone is quiet, the bills are somewhere else, and the dog does not need to be walked.

****

CHECKLIST ON DEVEOPING YOUR PLAYS

√ *Understand that development is about improving your play, period.*

√ *Be willing to experiment.*

√ *Take advantage of the chance to work with professionals.*

√ *Steal what you can.*

√ *Take the advice that makes sense, discard the rest.*

Marketing Your Play

Writers sometimes have a romantic image of themselves: the misunderstood genius, struggling for the truth among the Philistines. The fantasy involves the notion that someday someone will come along, read their stuff, declare them a genius, and then take care of them for the rest of their lives. Examine that proposition. It's the fantasy of an eight-year-old. Or else something made by MGM in the 30s. Same thing. Get over it. It ain't how the world works, and it really ain't how the theater works. There is no free lunch. Playwrights have to be grown-ups. Agents won't save us, producers won't save us, directors won't save us, and actors can't even think about saving us. And so we needs must save ourselves.

A word about agents before we proceed. Some playwrights are under the impression that if they get an agent, all their marketing problems will be solved. Wrong. Agents do not market your play for you. And there's an easy-to-understand reason why. There is not enough money to be made in the theater. Agents cannot afford to make blanket mailings of your play and long-distance phone calls and in general act like a Hollywood version of themselves. That postage and those phone bills are your responsibility. Agents function much more like lawyers. They help you with contracts and collect 10 percent of your royalties. And while they may be sweet to have around and their imprimatur on your play counts for something, they will not make your career.

That is your job. That is your job. That is your job.

Now to get an idea of what that job is and isn't. It is not putting manuscripts in the mail and waiting for a bite. That may be the relationship between other kinds of writers and their publishers. But it is not true of the relationship between playwrights and theaters. Playwrights should and do have more to do with the business than that. Theater is a collaborative art form, remember. And theaters really do like to know the playwrights they're working with. That means that you need to be out there seeing plays, meeting folks, participating in the acting and directing worlds.

A few of years ago, a friend spent eight hundred dollars sending out fifty copies of his newest play. Not a single production came from that. Not a single one. And it was a good play, too. When you figure that it costs about five bucks apiece to photocopy and bind your play and eight bucks apiece to get the thing out and back, that's thirteen dollars per copy. With thirteen dollars you could make a few phone calls, write a few letters, and generally increase your odds.

My friend's approach would be even less appropriate these days. Most theaters do not want you to send unsolicited material. Most of them want a synopsis, character breakdown, and ten sample pages of dialogue. And even then, it's a long shot that they will do your play. And so I would increase my chances by checking the website of any theater I was interested in. Make sure, first of all, that it does plays like yours. For example, if their house holds twelve hundred, they are not likely to do your two-person play set on a front porch. Likewise, if they did a Shakespeare, a Molière, and a musical last year, they're not going to be interested in your play, no matter how good it is. On the other hand, if they have a ninety-nine-seat house, no fly system, and an interest in realism or rural subjects, your front-porch play might be quite appropriate.

In general, however, you have to approach theaters and ask if you can send them a play. Don't leap off the edge without an invitation. Then it may be possible to send your play electronically. That saves money and time. Again, check to see if that's all right.

And now a few positive suggestions. Every city of moderate size has a few theaters. Go to them; see their productions—as many as possible. Choose the theaters with tastes like yours, and make appointments to talk to their literary managers. Folks in the theater are usually eager to know playwrights, particularly playwrights who live in the area.

This initial meeting shouldn't take long. You want to get a feel for the place and maybe drop off some work. Be smart about what they have done, and maybe in turn they will be smart about what you have done.

After that, you want to keep in touch with that theater and the person you met. Maybe that's a phone call every now and then. Maybe it's a note or an e-mail when you've seen something at their theater you liked. Maybe it's a postcard about a production of yours coming up. Then when you finish your next play, write a nice note and ask if you can send it along.

On a cautionary note, it's not wise to bug a theater about their opinion of what you sent. I always try to keep things friendly. If they don't say anything, it means no. And I'd just as soon not hear that; they'd also just as soon not say it. If we can both avoid discomfort, I feel easier about going back with my next play.

Yes, I am recommending a fairly personal approach to marketing. I do think it's the only way to go. I think also that playwrights who want access to a particular theater need to be aware of its work. It is both presumptuous and foolhardy to imagine that a theater will make the leap to get to know you if you won't first get to know them.

I've also been in the business for twenty years. I've had a hundred productions. Except for three or four of them, they were all the result of either a personal contact or a competition I'd won. That's a telling statistic, and it's similar for all the playwrights I know.

Now some other tactics. I would also suggest that you form relationships with a few directors. You do that the same way you form relationships with theaters. Know their work, arrange to meet them, then give them some of the your material, and keep in touch. Directors have their own relationships with theaters, and they are often asked to bring in projects. If your play is among the projects they recommend, your stock goes up, as do your chances of production.

I also recommend entering contests and applying to development labs, both of which need you. They are, after all, looking for new plays. Contests give you some money if you win and sometimes a production. Development labs give you actors, directors, and dramaturgs to work with. Often they give you invaluable help, and they always give you wonderful contacts.

By all means get a copy of *Dramatists Sourcebook*, published by Theatre Communications Group, 520 Eighth Avenue, New York, NY 10018-4156. This annual publication lists theaters, contests, publishers, development labs, agents, grants, colonies, membership organizations—everything a playwright would need a list of.

You might also consider joining the Playwrights' Center, a Minneapolis-based organization that provides support, development, and advocacy. It has a national membership and sends out frequent e-mail lists of playwriting opportunities. There are also other valuable development organizations. Check out those in your area of the country. It's also not a bad idea to join TCG (Theatre Communications Group). Membership comes with a journal, *American Theatre,* a useful publication for keeping up with current trends in the theater and periodic lists of productions at nonprofit theaters throughout the country. Finally I'd recommend joining the Dramatists Guild. This is our union. They publish a journal and a newsletter, but more importantly, they'll help members with free legal advice, a particularly useful thing if you don't have an agent.

Now a word about the long haul. Theaters presume that they will be around for a long time. You should presume the same thing. The networking goes on over time. Just because it doesn't yield something on the first play doesn't mean that it won't on future projects. In fact, don't even think of it in terms of a return. Think of your theater community in the same way you think of your family or your friends. You don't necessarily remember your aunt's birthday so that she'll give you something for Christmas. You remember it because you like your aunt. And that's enough in and of itself.

People in the theater are your professional family. You keep in touch, that's just what you do.

****

CHECKLIST FOR MARKETING

- √ Check websites of theaters you're interested in.
- √ See their work.
- √ Schedule time with people in those theaters.
- √ Develop relationships with directors.
- √ Enter contests and apply to development labs.
- √ Buy *Dramatists Sourcebook.*
- √ Keep in touch with your professional family.

These Are a Few of My Favorite Plays

What follows is my own idiosyncratic list of plays that have influenced me. I'm including only one play per playwright, and this list is not ordered in any particular way, but perhaps in the order one might have encountered them. What I'd advise is that we all make a list like this, just so we know whose shoulders we're standing on.

Athol Fugard, *Master Harold . . . and the Boys*
Caryl Churchill, *Cloud Nine*
William Shakespeare, *Hamlet*
Suzan-Lori Parks, *American Play*
Julia Jordan, *Tatanja in Color*
Carter Lewis, *Women Who Steal*
Beth Henley, *Crimes of the Heart*
Samuel Beckett, *Waiting for Godot*

Dael Orlander Smith, *Yellow Man*
David Hare, *Plenty*
David Greenburg, *Three Days of Rain*
Marsha Norman, *'night, Mother*
David Henry Abair, *Kimberly Akimbo*
Julie Jensen, *Two-Headed*
Franz Kreutz, *Through the Leaves*
Edward Albee, *Who's Afraid of Virginia Woolf?*
August Wilson, *Fences*
David Mamet, *American Buffalo*
Tom Stoppard, *Rozencrantz and Guildenstern Are Dead*
Adam Bock, *Swimming in the Shallows*
Eugene Ionesco, *The Bald Soprano*
John Webster, *The Duchess of Malfi*
Moliere, *Tartuffe*
Lisa Kron, *Well*
Sarah Ruhl, *Clean House*
Alfred Uhry, *Driving Miss Daisy*
Thornton Wilder, *Our Town*
David Storey, *Home*
Sam Shepard, *True West*
Oscar Wilde, *The Importance of Being Earnest*
Jean Genet, *The Maids*
Aeschylus, *The Oresteia*
Luis Alfaro, *Bitter Homes and Gardens*
Anne Commire, *Put Them All Together*
Paula Cizmar, *Street Stories*

Martin Sherman, *Bent*
Wendy Wasserstein, *The Heidi Chronicles*
Jean Claude van Itallie, *America Hurrah*
Ntozake Shange, *For Colored Girls Who Have Considered Suicide/When the Rainbow Is Not Enuf*
John Guare, *House of Blue Leaves*
David Henry Hwang, *M-Butterfly*
Lanford Wilson, *Fifth of July*
David Rabe, *Streamers*
Craig Lucas, *Blue Window*
Mac Wellman, *Seven Blow Jobs*
Lee Breuer, *Gospel at Colonus*
Mary Zimmerman, *Arabian Knights*
John Osborne, *Look Back in Anger*
Jay Presson Allen, *The Prime of Miss Jean Brodie*
Lorraine Hansberry, *Raisin in the Sun*
Zora Neal Hurston, *Mule Bone*
Horton Foote, *Trip to Bountiful*
Preston Jones, *The Texas Trilogy*
Tony Kushner, *Angels in America*
Eugene O'Neill, *Long Day's Journey into Night*
Doug Wright, *I Am My Own Wife*
Tenessee Williams, *Glass Menagerie*
Arthur Miller, *Death of a Salesman*
Paula Vogel, *Baltimore Waltz*
Christopher Marlowe, *Edward II*
Charles Ludlam, *The Mystery of Irma Vep*
Simon Gray, *Butley*

LeRoi Jones, *Dutchman*
Tina Howe, *Painting Churches*
Spalding Gray and James Strahs, *Point Judith*
Amy Freed, *The Beard of Avon*
Irene Fornes, *The Conduct of Life*
Plays by The Lesbian Brothers
Plays by The Wooster Group

Afterword

All right, now you know as much as I do. And of course, I believe that's all you need to know. So there's nothing else to do but get to work. With my blessing.

ABOUT THE AUTHOR

Julie Jensen was reared in southern Utah. She has a PhD in theater from Wayne State University in Detroit and has taught playwriting at seven different colleges and universities. She worked as a writer in Hollywood for five years and until recently directed the graduate playwriting program at the University of Nevada, Las Vegas. She is now Resident Playwright at Salt Lake Acting Company.

Jensen is the recipient of the Kennedy Center Award for New American Plays (*White Money*), the Joseph Jefferson Award for Best New Work (*The Lost Vegas Series*), and the LA Weekly Award for Best New Play (*Two-Headed*). She has received the McKnight National Playwriting Fellowship (*WAIT!*), the TCG/NEA Playwriting Residency (*WAIT!*), and a major grant from the Pew Charitable Trusts (*Dust Eaters*). She has won the Mill Mountain Theater Playwriting Competition three times (*Tender Hooks, Last Lists of My Mad Mother,* and *Two-Headed*). Her play, *Two-Headed*, was included in the volume *Women Playwrights: The Best Plays of 2000*, she has twice been nominated by the American Theater Critics Association for the best new play produced outside New York (*Last Lists of My Mad Mother* and *Dust Eaters*), and she was a finalist for the PEN USA Award for Drama (*Dust Eaters*).

Her work has been produced in London and at the Edinburgh Fringe Festival as well as in New York and theaters nationwide. She has been commissioned by Mark Taper Forum, ASK Theater Projects, Kennedy Center, Actors Theater of Louisville, Salt Lake Acting Company, Geva Theater, and Philadelphia Theater Company. Her work is published by Dramatic Publishing, Dramatists Play Service, Playscripts, Inc., Heinemann, and Smith and Kraus, Inc.